; Or,

How We Stopped Warming Up for 20 Years and Learned to Exit the Green Room

; Or,

How We Stopped Warming Up for 20 Years and Learned to Exit the Green Room

VARIOUS AUTHORS

POETRY ARCHIVES 1993–2013

Curated and Edited by Leah Angstman

Violet Ray SERIES

Alternating Current Press
Boulder, Colorado

; Or, How We Stopped Warming Up for 20 Years
and Learned to Exit the Green Room
Various Authors
©*1993–2013, 2020* Alternating Current

Alternating Current
Boulder, Colorado
alternatingcurrentarts.com

ISBN: 978-1-946580-24-5
First Collected Edition: August 2020

Letter from the Editor
LEAH ANGSTMAN

In 1993, I was a pre-teen, cutting and pasting together newsprint zines and photo-copied chapbooks in a sprawled-out chaos on my parents' living room floor. The story of how this printing venture started is old now, as are a lot of the teen-written first publications that launched this publishing house—some cringeworthily out-dated and childish. But some of them are the good, solid pieces that defined the zine era at the turn of the millennium and captured the "outlaw poetry" scenes of Los Angeles, New York, San Francisco, and the Midwest. With the norm being submissions by snail mail and purchases by trade, it was the age of advertisement swaps, handmade broadsides, penpal friendship books, add-on and pass-on sheets, zine-exchange chain letters, pop-up poetry readings, open mics, and book festivals plopped unannounced under tents on the corner without a permit. A lot of it was worth letting go, but the good stuff is worth preserving and revisiting.

This collection is the good stuff that kicked off our press, preserved and archived here for more than the literary scholar or the nostalgically curious—it's presented here because the work is truly worth revisiting. We didn't republish *everything*; we cut what needed to be cut from the middle-school opinions and freshman first-love poetry sagas, and we emerged with the pieces that came from those who, at the time, were adults peddling their refined wares in the marketplace of zinedom whose work deserves to be read. You'll see some of the same names over and over again, from the self-proclaimed *ol' bearded bard* John Binns to the erotic, sexual, and über-fem-when-it-was-mightily-frowned-upon Laura Joy Lustig—those who were prominent in the scene and provided us with new material year after year—and you'll see a couple of one-poet wonders, who have since gone the way of pre-email long-lost and long-moved-away and no-longer-in-college-dorms mailing addresses. This is what survived the archival file fires, what we're proud to have captured, and what we're proud to pass on.

While this anthology comprises several early editions, this is the first time these pieces, previously only found in out-of-print photocopied chapbooks, newsprint zines, and disappeared social-profile blogs, have ever appeared in paperback print and entirely together. The anthology combines photocopied books without ISBNs, spanning from 1997 to 2007, with single straggler pieces from various projects spanning from 1993 to 2013. The included publications, now in paperback for the first time, with their pieces published in the order they were originally published, are: *Crackrock #1* (November 1997), *Crackrock #2* (August 1998), *Real-Life Poet* (January 1999), *The Literature Collection* (July 1999), *Punctuation* (2002), *Broken Livers & Broken Lives* (1996–2006), *Avenues & Parking Lots* (2006), and the Myspace online netzine *Medusa* (2006–2007). All of those are long-gone and will never be republished as they once were (you're welcome, I promise)—this is now the only place that you can find these fantastic archived publications and pieces.

These were our beautiful, (funny), humble beginnings. This is why we started this whole mess. This, *this*, is why we're still here. Because it's something worth revisiting, every time.

"We shape our buildings;
thereafter, our buildings
shape us."
—Winston Churchill

Table of Contents

POETRY

THE LITERATURE COLLECTION — JULY 1999

The Jaws of Hell Beckoned

JOHN BINNS

Well, I feel poetic,
So I will tell
Of a trip I nearly took
Into the jaws of hell.

Well, it was one dark night
When I was way-uptight
And the jaws of hell beckoned,
And I would have
Fallen in, I reckon,
If I had not drawn back
And avoided a lack
That I will never have again
For now I have a brain.

Bad Blood and Bittersweets

IRIS BERRY

This is for all of you
all the x-friends
friends that never were
and x-boyfriends.
For all of you
whom I don't speak to
and who don't speak to me.
For all the hurt feelings and broken hearts,
parking tickets unpaid,
and monies unreturned.
Apartments trashed
and cars crashed.
Windows broken and memoirs stolen.
Evictions and aborted infidelities.
Skipped bail and unanswered mail.
All the black-eyed, bloodstained
dirty laundry,
all the times I pissed you off
and you me.
This is for all of you,
all the broken souls and poked holes.
Well, I can't be your voodoo doll,
and you can't be mine.
I've closed my eyes,
and it didn't go away,
there wasn't a day that went by
where I didn't feel,
and the nights I lost sleep
for every one of you
and you me.
And we know it.
And we live with the ghosts of the still-living,
ghosts with unused telephone numbers.
Yet we don't call,

we don't try,
and we don't say,
and it's not the tragedies that tore us apart,
it's what happens after that keeps us away.
And maybe if there were a crisis,
we'd talk
and say how we wasted so much time
and how we're sorry.
And we are just that,
so sorry.

No Angels Up My Cunt

LAURA JOY LUSTIG

i'd give up
both boyfriends
& one really comfortable
pair of shoes
for one good head
w/ reason and accomplishment enough
for great paintings/
poems
to justify habitual cigarette smoking
& the fucking of dumb boys
w/ incredibly manicured face
that make sense of my drinking
that try to make me
piss in glee
on rooftops.
presuming our happiness
is the same
—making me itch instead
w/ red hives & atomic
allergic reactions
to illiterate card-buyers
& 1-800-flower givers.
romantic prerequisite
spins plastic card-holders only
and nothing else
but one for the sky ...
to always believe those believers
who say all they want is ...
to be loved.
know what this means.
it says nothing
about loving you.
rid fairytales & chorus.
save unwanted precious breaths

from modern hair-do's
that still believe vagina
is love-canal/
spiritually transcendent.
no angels up my cunt
nor enlightenment upon admission.
just plainly overdone
& simply just that.
vagina is not
center.
sex
is not love.
more like
jump rope.

Where's the Woman At?

JIM DEWITT

with everyday life just dragging along
she feels like a piece of wheat
at a rice convention
and long ago ceased doing what had helped
in past-memory years, now simply licking
a finger to hold up
to see which way the wind is

her today's state of mind coming from
former wifehood is
am I just good for picking over
in the marketplace of a downtown bar?
going there for emotional refueling
every once in a while
like searching for that skinny gigolo
quick fix on Florida Keys beaches

hear tiny faraway voices saying
watch out watch out you'll just end up
red meat meant for the beasts' appetites
pass oh please pass
you concrete-slab-colored days

yes she is willing to wait it out
till finally big old nature
decides to pay her a special visit
to dapple her sky the way she likes best

Pray to the Cherries

LAURA JOY LUSTIG

marvelous—
if cherries were answers
to universal contemplations.
and pits—
unanimous explanation
for such inquiries.
they'd give realization
to wasted time
presuming s/thing greater/
insulting simplicity.
—first mistakes are looking.
often too many greats
go unseen.
the cherries are inside.
small.
modest.
mistaken for grapes
& stomped with feet
looking for greater
on top shelves
of lonely aisles
w/ empty
dust/
academia
beside.

The Age-Old Way

JOHN BINNS

Get some work done
And forget about the bun
That you feel you should have,
And go to the lav
When you feel the need,
But don't smoke that weed,
No, put it out
And develop some clout
In the age-old way
And your good times will stay.

See Stray Dragoons in the Hollow

JIM DEWITT

"drudgery is the first law
of the universe" sayeth the whitemaned sage
scarfing a mouth-to-full with catfish
& not even pierced ears
can convert blokes
into dreamers of sorts, so the sensation
of straight gin on non-rocks
won't puncture one's workaholic sleep
sure as the North Pole's really
a red & white spiral ...
but "do tote that barge, savior"
for the mostest relief omen becomes
a muscle massage
& then it's a quick chuga beer
for the road because your econobox car
is just itching to meet
that-there oak in a faceoff

Stuff ét.

LAURA JOY LUSTIG

i want to be
where poetry intervals
are at minimum
even & especially so
when inspiration
parades unpleasantly.
the stronger the feeling
the bigger the poem's nostril.
happiness is easily amused
& chronically weak.
puke goes well
w/ typing paper.
& smiles are for kitties
or those who don't know
& are better off not knowing
they think
—so therefore they are not/
or at least at minimum too
where humans are degrees
& best bets are to never
say i think TOO MUCH
(in pathetic attempt to shut me up)
—it's my job/
& what separates our nature
into human
and ...
lesser ...
—never, too,
sound interested
immediately post-daydreams.
i know where you were/
love pop quizzes
& don't forgive too easily
but nonetheless do often enough
of pity & boredom.
so rest sweet dumb beauty
i'll click nerve cells on heels/

make love in tubes
—it's the motion i dig.
make me feel good. bad. s/thing live
because everything else is dead.
there is no 1st or preferable anything
so boys AND girls
take men out backs
read some poems
on knees
past discomfort
to know worship
is greatest gift-giver
directly feeding soul
w/ no quick bank statements.

The Love Drug

J. PALEY

The Drug, not the user, is known to be the master.
From the first moment that you inject yourself into me,
I am your slave.
Your hypnotic scent curls into my nostrils
and numbs my brain with icy fingers.
Your soothing tongue slips down my throat
and churns my stomach with one flick of your barbed tail.
Your wish has become my command;
your desire, my reality.
There is no turning back.
No erasing my many mistakes.
No righting my many wrongs.
You have pulled me under the wave
and drained all life from me,
leaving me lying on the unforgiving sand,
my veins full of holes,
and my eyes streaked with red snakes.
I know that you are bad for me.
That you are killing me.
But I can't break away
because I am hopelessly addicted to You.

Ask Your Dad

God knows
How your garden grows,
And he is aware
Of the tares in your hair,
So look lively lad!
And ask your dad
If you want to know
How his garden grows,
For he has a point of view
And he will tell it to you
If you are not too proud
And not too loud
To listen to him
And stop being a quim.

An Exit Waiting to Happen

IRIS BERRY

I've hung from the rafters
and swung from the chandeliers
bounced off the walls
and been thrown down the stairs.
I've been
banned
canned
shammed
and damned.
86'd
thrown out
and thrown against the wall.
I've been under the table
and overthrown.
I've left out the bathroom window
the back door
and been asked to leave
at gunpoint.
I've lost just about everything
I ever loved and cared for
had it smashed to pieces
or thrown out of 4th story windows
at 4 a.m. in the rain.
My specialty,
dramatic exits.
My problem,
not knowing
when it's time to go.

Storm Trooper of the Judicial System

JIM DEWITT

The godlike figure you seek
in back of that
imposing District Court desk
they respectfully call "Magistrate"
because any and all
reasonable evidence you present
no matter how logical
will be legally turned against you
so-help-you clever
God Of Trust at work ...
and better be prepared to believe it
pre-gavel slam
you'll be declared
GUILTY UNTIL PROVEN GUILTY
as long as your hopeful mouth
shall plead.

What?

JOHN BINNS

What have they got
To shout about?
A wife? A husband?
Some silly lout
Who goes to the bookie's
And drinks beer
And for them I will not
Shed no tear
For they have only
Themselves to blame
If they are
Caught up in the game.

The Job

LAURA JOY LUSTIG

to fuck
& flirt
w/ all bedraggled
creative-type boys
w/ s/ great heads/
s/ small dicks/
never whole smiles—
admiringly knowing
all impossibilities.
to give bits
of beauty
to ea.
& pull back/
watch bodily cataclysm/
mercurial head permutation
& say only beauty is fair enough exchange
of this unpleasant kind.
think of all poems/
paintings/unsound experiments
that could not exist
solely on happiness.
(CAUSE too weak!)
my job & excuse are the same
to thank me later for endings now
& to know balance
is range.

Fast and Far

PINGUINO

Don't take this the wrong way, but you know too much—
Stay till the 2nd, when you were supposed to go.
Just stay another night. You'll devastate people—Stay Stay Stay—
    Trembling and terrified,
    Seeking comfort in the arms of the news bearer.
    Whom to trust; the world spins inversely.
    What is trust when it's ignored when the boat splinters apart.
They are out there, trying to come in—Stop Being Paranoid—
They want to kill—Fearless of disposable bodies—
It Was Just An Accident—They want to kill
    To kill one who was once a friend, or a trusted acquaintance,
    What is trust when you jump to conclusions?
I drive fast and far, stopping for gas—Wait—
    The gas cap won't come off. Struggling sleepily with an object
    Like getting childproof caps off in the middle of the night.
    The key doesn't fit any longer.
    A hundred miles from home.
    Stranded—I Got Lucky—Asking for help
People feel pity and the gas cap is forcefully removed.
    They're insane; wanted to leave me in the desert for the
    Truckers and cacti and snakes and inbred hicks to find—
    They wanted me to stay—
    I got lucky.
    Are they following me? What car is that?
    What state are the plates?
    I duck down in my seat and drive,
    Never been hunted before.
    The game isn't fun anymore.
Each car that passes increases my nervousness. I duck a lot.
    People must think I'm a weirdo.
    Good, more of the road for me.
Thinking hurts a lot.
    Especially when your perceptions of friends and friendship
    Within an hour
    Warp into the purest form of terror imaginable.
It's weird knowing people want your existence erased
    Just because you know too much,

Because they trusted you then changed their minds.
You can't move files in the human brain.
I drive fast and far, past the state line,
Glad I didn't stay an hour longer,
I smile.
Giddy explosive laughter—I Made It—Everything will be okay
They didn't follow.
I'm still here.
A new adventure lies ahead.

On with the Hunt

JOHN BINNS

It is off we go,
With a tally-ho
And an on with the hunt,
And a set of silly cunts.

What I Do

LAURA JOY LUSTIG

is s/thing like
dictating fingers—
fornicating
& experienced.
kidding themselves
silly—
when words
go too fast
in the head.

To Ensure Worth-While

LAURA JOY LUSTIG

1. mourn nothing
because all is already gone
& essentially there is no
nothing.
just severe inquisition
on unlawful double-negatives.

believe, have faith—hope
if you must.
but know
you appear only as
incomprehensible as you are.

2. feel guilty—never—
because i master that void
& you'll never get answers
to questions on functions.

parents and blue-balls
will try & try again.

3. never think settling
in any other way than house.

never feel it permissible
according to popular
biological spinster deadlines.

4. never, ever feel comfortable/
trust w/ all of anyone's heart
& dive sense first—
not only do you risk absurdity
but you may be deceived

—& i'd rather meet death
than watch myself kill
my deceiver.
—nothing is more alienating.
wounded truths are blasts
compared to those blows.

think performance
before romance—
he's getting paid
by the show.
passion
is pre-installed/
set at eyes
w/ formulated "i love you's"
& similar tribe.

o. kill. & forgive a lot less/
force unpleasant brain-surge
in masturbating head-slackers
that think everything's cool.

A Thirsty Earth's First Recipe

JIM DEWITT

Jenny's teeny skip-steps
turn tricks of light for any
bona fide pedophile
to slurp his chops lusting after
her tongue-untouched appleblossom winner ...
how its hopscotch haunts him
whispering to a pervert self
smiled behind lacy-curtain lures
encouraging "achievement"
and such performing like heatcrazed
lovers licking off
tweedled fingers oozing ice creamy
from a melting-passion act
of any occasion's summer.

The Rimes Simply Stop

JOHN BINNS

I like to be out
But I have my doubts
About the weather of late,
For sometimes it's great,
But at other times
The rimes
Simply stop
Or flop.

Cocktail Knowledge

IRIS BERRY

The men's room.
The ladies' powder room.
Locker room,
off color,
poker party,
shop talk.
Backstage.
Burlesque house,
after hours,
closing time.
VIP.
X-rated,
censored and unabridged.
Cocktail knowledge.
An education
in itself.

Guided by an Elf

PINGUINO

walking through the hazy memories
losing my soul kissing away my past
loosening the ties to this place
a pull yet another
tiny strands holding me back
holding me down
responsibility

snaking around my tired body
cutting into numb wasted flesh
it blossoms and flowers
freshly watered with love

yin yang tangarang
follow the yellow brick road?
follow follow follow follow
follow the yellow brick road

On the Ship of Dreams

JOHN BINNS

On the ship of dreams
There are piebald schemes
To work your way at,
But most folks just play at
The things they have,
And they go to the lav,
And they get stuck in-
To the rotgut gin,
And in a while
They cease to smile.

First Night to Not Sleep over the New Man's House

LAURA JOY LUSTIG

i swear
(b/c i don't have a hell to be condemned)
all i took
was way too much.
a ceiling fan TICK
a stream of too-bright sun
on early sat. morn.
a late-night roommate yapping
& a bit of the old snore-in-ear fun.
i was ready to leave
grab the bra & out
go back to the old cock
& never look back.
sure the old one wasn't as big
but it was indeed nighttime friendly.
this was perfectly justifiable
in all manners.
problem is
i never sat too well
w/ 2 cocks
at 1 time
even if it was
a wk. stretch bt. intervals.
rather know
1 cock
at 1 time
to acquire fit & taste
than be ½-ass
w/ both.

Return to Six One Nine

PINGUINO

My wallet fluctuates in weight
The ever-present chain dragging along
Digits in my account decrease
We're dragging each other down
Days away from hitting concrete
Harsh reality smacks us around
Scrambling to salvage our lifestyle
We gather our meager possessions
Losing sleep while racking our brains
A week is spent in scurried packing
Our options dwindling down to one
Return home and admit defeat
My personal goals hardly obtained
A slave to comfort, tied to age
My hope lies within a creative venture
Winding through the printing press
My savings the responsibility of others
As I wait for my production to release
My creation lets me prove myself
That advertising has taught me much
Pride from my friends and family
Is a key element that I seek
To unlock confidence hidden within
Yet I know that even if I returned
Empty-handed, devastated, and alone
That I would still be loved and accepted
And that's what defines my home.

You Will Go Blind

JOHN BINNS

Time,
Why worry?
And why hurry
All around the place
With a grimace
Upon your face,
When empty space
Is all you will find?
And you will go blind
If that you seek,
Is this of which I speak.

Trash

J. J. CAMPBELL

digging through the trash
any street corner
any big city

they are looking for the america
they read about
the one they saw in the movies
the apple pies
the wealth
the streets full of gold
and names in neon

instead they are rummaging
for french fries
discarded cigarettes
waiting for the better off
to come off a few coins
so that one day
they can buy a meal

but unlike most of us
they haven't quit
they don't think of themselves
as failures
and when they look
in the mirror each day
they don't think about suicide

they just look at it as
another day the
american dream may come true

unlike us
this is not as good as the rest
mass of society

we look in the mirror each day
with no hope
no dreams
praying that a random bullet
has our name on it

Demented Whips Gouge

JIM DEWITT

It's time. Red drizzle dropping gouts.
Your cue to howl on down and visit my
lair. Mutually in our hunger for pain

we'll play "enslave me." Hurry. Schem-
ing all the while for vicious second
chances. Altered like ravenous were-

wolves lick victims. We'll be laced
gloriously into slavering blue-hemp
ghosts gorging their hearts out on our

cankered limbs gone pallid. Tastier
than the Worm of Malice could ever
know. And while in disguise we'll be

attacking our own sanity with razor-
edge wings. Delightfully to be torturing
hideous alien souls so fragile they

can no longer conjure these peel-off
disguises.

Poem Found

LAURA JOY LUSTIG

found this.
kept it for s/ time now.
wasn't doing much w/ it though.
realized this is what i need—
s/one to give of myself & the material
things that s/how transcribe the message beneath
bright colors & brilliant complements.
i need s/one that
i like & can give my junk to.

The Bell

PINGUINO

Linenoise, a tiny kitten,
oddly striped, mewing in the pet store,
leaping out each time the cage opened.
He was chosen and given as a gift
of love, and the kitten returned the love.
A tiny bell hung about his neck.
It jingled and we knew he was okay.
Whether he was in the closet or under the bed
or inside the couches or under the stereo,
the bell told us where to find him.
Father Time changed the kitten
into a beautiful cat, who snuggled close
and soaked in knowledge and memories.
One day, Linenoise's collar was not tightened.
The bell and collar fell off, never to be seen again.
Linenoise did not understand.
He moped and he brooded, hiding himself away.
The jingle that complemented his every move
nonexistent. He aged and grew distant.
His toys remained in place, with no
soft paws to bat them beyond human view.
And then a noise teased the cat's ears,
a bell, so similar to his own,
yet his paws padded along silently.
Realizing Linenoise's need and noticing
the missing bell and collar,
a new bell was located
and hung around Linenoise's neck.
He played again, frolicked, and danced.
He slept on shoulders and laps
as if nothing had been out of place.
Who would think a bell,
an item of decoration and shine,
could affect an animal so greatly
that he took it as a sign of age,
a seemingly human concept
displayed in feline fancy.

Soup of Titles I Thought Mix

LAURA JOY LUSTIG

born
lotsa-yesterdays-ago
& at every turn
i stayed
faithful
always washing my ass
w/ ivory/
never the scented stuff/
airing the penis
w/ nothing other than
picasso—
(only the best!)
even though
i never had a penis
but s/x tried.
most days
would be travel
on going mad
& feeling it easy
& others—
accepting
a very large
clitoris
for the immediate
control.

Nobody Likes a Quitter

J. J. CAMPBELL

i have a friend who told me
once she tried to kill herself
by taking a whole bottle of tylenol

and unlike most kids
of our generation
she didn't quit when she failed
she kept on trying

she tried a total of four times
the last being five years ago

and i give her shit
from time to time
when she starts
talking about death

i tell her nobody likes a quitter

and my conscience asks me
would i feel guilty
if she did kill herself

and i tell my conscience no
i wouldn't feel guilty

i'd just be pissed that
she wasn't kind enough
to invite me along
for the ride

The Sacred Truth

JOHN BINNS

Off to the left
I see people bereft,
And off to the right
I see people uptight,
And in the middle
I have to piddle
On the sacred truth
That makes them uncouth.

An Ash Can Burns at the Feet of Christ

JULIAN GALLO

Through the iron bars
beneath the paint-stuck windows
along littered dirty streets
amongst the rat-infested playgrounds
there is a voice crying out
a voice being heard but not
listened to
a voice in pain
an incantation lost in the howling winds
of apathy and indifference
verbal regurgitations bathed in streetlight
and cloaked in maniacal laughter
There are eyes looking through those
grimy windows
looking down at the wasteland
of human endeavor

In the back alleys of Jerusalem
a prophet lies naked
drunk and covered in sick
pissing against a brick wall
and gazing at the stars
which seem dim over the skies
of New York City
but bright in the hearts of every man
woman and child who still has hope—
a cheap dime-store dream
washed down with a glass of water
scooped out of the East River

The prophet snores through the
immolation of desires
immolation of lives
immolation of dreams
where pint-sized Al Capones
draw their guns, deal their dope
and crush the dreams of children
who sit on sandstone stoops
and rusted fire escapes
counting the stars they see
as blotches on their future

Whores fuck and pimps are getting paid
Whores dance among the orgasms
and suck off the lonely men
who wander the asphalt desert in search
of a meaning
In the dark alley, an ash can burns
at the feet of Christ
and His shadow shimmers on the wall
amongst the graffiti
and scriptures of the urban prophets
too hungry or dopesick to
give a shit about the clouded jewels
on His crown of thorns

And I hear your voice in the
night, a whisper
faint and sweet
and I feel your presence
in my heart and see
your eyes in the dark
feel your pumping heart
and loving hands
opening the window to my soul

And despite the scenery outside the window
you are the shining light that illuminates
the world

Assertive Man Said:

LAURA JOY LUSTIG

"i know
you
love me/
just
not sure
that is
all
you want"

A Minor Apocalypse
JULIAN GALLO

Some fear war
some fear death, disease
some fear losing everything
some fear the shadows under the bed
some fear the skeletons in the closet
will one day rattle out
some fear intimacy
some fear love
some fear losing face
some fear sex, violence, and punishment
some fear failure
some fear success
some fear losing the child
nestled against their breast
some fear criticism
some fear praise
some fear responsibility
while others fear laziness and slack
some fear hate
some fear being shut out
while others eat the cake

What I fear is
the minor apocalypse
that occurs whenever I get close
to you

Sexual Sneezes

JIM DEWITT

sure was glad she blurted
"time to liven up, let there be
more pepper in our love"
because immediately
that nudged me to tote in
a potent supply
sprinkled it liberally into this vixen's
major swale ... talk about your
spasms incited
lasting for hours, primitive pizzazz
we'd never known before
snorting thunder of the all-night
rocking kind couldn't
let itself up
till we felt some slow beams oozing in
from the sunrise side
of the hill

When We Get Some Rain

JOHN BINNS

Sweet reason comes to me,
And I can see
A bit further,
But does he lurk
Here, the berk
Whom I pursue?
And is he gunning for you,
You who
Are pure?
Well, the cure
Is plain,
And when we get some rain,
It will cleanse my brain
And stop me from going insane.

Now Serving Number ...

J. J. CAMPBELL

i've stopped counting the number
of friends of mine who have died

it just depressed me too much
to know that the number was higher
than the amount of years
i've lived on this planet

and there are days when i've thought
about adding my name
to that ever-growing list

but i realize that's a silly notion
especially when i remember
who my friends are

they're just like me

they've stopped
counting as well

The Difference of Words & Motion

LAURA JOY LUSTIG

one moves
the other doesn't.
one is
as other
supposes to be.
know
i want
s/one
who wants
me
always
but
need
s/thing
more
than
s/one
just
mouthing
it

The Ghost of Charlie Parker Blows Chunks through His Hypodermic Horn

JULIAN GALLO

Funny.
There's a phenomenon occurring
these days—nothing new unfortunately
but it's everywhere you look
The death of youth
The death of creativity and potential
genius

On the streets of the Lower East Side
the foot soldiers of a new generation
are waging war against the self
all in the name of art and the ever-elusive
"cool"

Heroin—the new creative blood
a nihilistic nourishment
to quench the thirst of idiots
and the creative minds of the inane

The ghost of Charlie Parker blows chunks
through his hypodermic horn
and you bathe in it, a baptism for a new
vision

Wading in the sick
seeking
immortality

Funny.

Last time I looked, immortality
was written on the pages
in the legend of their own minds.

An Ode
Post-Reading Mr. Buk

LAURA JOY LUSTIG

words
have gotten us drunk/
disagreeable
w/ anti-extremists
w/o ever knowing
abundance
to see it good or
otherwise.
but we dig it anyway
like TOO much sounds/
go to libraries for hours
just to bite
one good nail
—make cuticles
smooth
w/ rough files
of teeth
thinking—
being
next to no one
better
than bored
in school
knowing
reading is good
w/o utilitarianism
governing.
rather be taxi driver
than talk shakespeare in bookshop
(but still insist the option)
—faster make it bloody
than allow presupposed look
from hunting man's nose
sniffing all methods

no science/
never sex—
thinks that's dirty too.
rather be that taxi-chick
than professor
w/ constant worry
of proper head-tilt
to pre-assigned behavior
well-knowing
interests would be broad
if rare was/
murder not so prolific.
power is the acceptance
of challenge
not the temporal
destruction/
sitting arm-raised
wide-mouthing every drip

God

J. J. CAMPBELL

there's been some impressive
lightning around here
the last two nights
and i have this fetish
to go outside and watch it
while smoking a cigarette

well, last night
one bolt hit in the field
behind me and another
hit in the field across the street

when i saw this happen
i stepped out into the rain
and said to god
"you missed asshole"
i then stuck my arms out
taunting him to hit me

i told my friend about it
and he said i was nuts
for fucking with the lord like that

to which i replied
"god doesn't have the balls
to kill me. besides, he knows
some other motherfucker
is bound to do it for him
one day."

Done Wasted Be That Chance

JIM DEWITT

Poison tears drive at my peace's neck.
Chunk colors to drive any throat to
disruption. Makes me twist all of
Satan's loves unto myself.
How much joy is there in self-
hammering? Breathing dark sludge down
your hollow place gone yellow? You
know, scaly hard-rock beats can scathe
sharp hate going deeper.
No more of that fending off of "cute"
chaos claiming penetration. But if
you dare blocking my mania trend, I'll
fuck over five more of your former
boyfriends.
Even chance compound fractures by
refusing to pass through the gamut. You
and your sadistic by-play of self-
satisfaction.

Random House Ology

LAURA JOY LUSTIG

twizzler
sticks
& such bionic
proportions
cut cesarean
divas
open like
carnivore monthlies.
& i smile
b/c comics are poets—
getting laughs from truth/
still brave enough
to dive
& i smile
& never really mean it
b/c all is freed
when it never can really
be.
space & time
exist
barely to the mouth
w/ little escape/
beside mind
play/
which i foster—
so bare it.

Petty Little Arguments

J. J. CAMPBELL

why do couples
find it necessary
to include me
in their petty little arguments
like i need their shit
piled on top of my own
and then they have the nerve
to ask me
who's right
who won

i just tell them
there are no winners
at these silly games
only survivors
and sometimes
surviving
ain't all it's
cracked up to be

Since I Cannot Break Your Knees

JIM DEWITT

as would a telemarketer-hating
pestmutt, I must
(figuratively of course) snarlingly
bite onto your salespitch-retreating
ass cuz meanwhile the
ever-shifting gyre of your
remote callousness keeps the fluff
of your phony face
away from availability.
Merely a cattle thief's in modernized
Jurassic mode, slinking further
from honest toil.
And made for malingering
among the worst like-minds
of your generation.

Lies

JOHN BINNS

The lies they tell
And the seeds they sell
In the name of the law
Or some crashing bore
Of an idea which
Is for the mighty rich,
While those who seek to find
Some peace of mind
Will ignore all this
And plump for a kiss.

Right / Left? – "Yeah"

LAURA JOY LUSTIG

i think
therefore i think i am.
one can never be too sure
of any one thing.
descartes tells me
that's why i am
w/o even asking me
if i ever wanted to be.
cool-dig-sartre says
i'm never not thinking.
& according to s/ —
double-negatives are quite displeasing/
almost blasphemous.
so smile.   fuck.   dance.
when observing this idiocy.
such sticky tips of fingers
& know s/x taste is yummy/
guilt—
never so charmed.
i think too
b/c it's more dangerous
than fucking
& at x's
equal to such philosophies.
s/x fucking
is simply just that
& that bores the fuck/
dick/
right slopping-flipping
outta me.
if only we could simultaneously
know/preach & screw
living ideas
never amputated ...
... they must be fucked
& in no manner wasted.
make it come

grind slut-ass hips. nurture.
those w/ no mind
concentrate
between thighs.
absolute maintains only
two types:
those of constant flux
& those where it is already assumed
you arose from sleep this morning
if you later
wrote the song/did the dance
to pretty poem.
just another ode
to killing poets slowly
w/ no logic/
little else.

Anything Baby

IRIS BERRY

I'd go to
the ends
of the earth
and East L.A.
I'd spend
the rest
of my life
on the Ventura Fwy.
I'd do hard time,
I'd scrub hard floors.
Hell Vietnam,
I'd fight three wars.
I'd commit myself
gladly to Bellevue
and all the ink spots
would look like you.
I'd sleep with Manson
and the Hillside Strangler,
I'd drink Drano, Comet,
and hair detangler.
I'd do anything short
of turning blue,
anything baby
to get away from you.

Relationships

LAURA JOY LUSTIG

often
like
the relay race
—one dirty stick
exchange
w/ little intermission/
one worn woman
until
time
is up

Dead Is Good if You Don't Know How to Properly Be Alive

LAURA JOY LUSTIG

talk 2
& squeeze
bush
tight./
above ground
w/ bones below.
pelvis.
—inside its earth
where everyone above
loves 2 play psychic
w/
& say they are
"@ peace"
2 cover
pre-death asses/
prolific
living allusion.
will
is
never enough—
there is no
miraculous roads
unless sprinkled w/
milk & hashish
—everyone has yielded
@ signs
they've made yellow
while language made
purposefully
universally
unrecognizable.

& 1 dead man
gives more peace
than whole
outfits
of above-grounders
not burnt
or
frozen.

Beware

GIOVANNI MALITO

Does memory matter
and is sentiment real?
What is guilt? And why
does he feel guilty
when he says he misses
the rhythm of the washboard?
They say bruises never heal
but beware those cuts
that do not bleed—
they are telling you something.

No Tragic Ending

JOHN BINNS

And to those rehearsing dying
I have only this to say,
Are you sure that life has ended
And the dream has flown away?
In the Garden of Gethsemane
They come for you each day,
But there will be no tragic ending
To my own immortal play.

The Cage

JIM DEWITT

what triggers her to burst into chuckles
at the slightest provocation
they're a strange sort of cross between
a cluck and a chirp
not too ladylike but so what
because she keeps herself to empty rooms
for the most part (except for the cage)—
her "laughing" sound being a cawing bellow
bouncing off walls and ceiling
"that sure is a good one, eh?" she'll say
knowing no neighbor is there listening ...
then she'll go flying down
the corridor, her laughter rising in echo
to almost terrifying screech-pitch
till the furthest door bursts out
a Jack-of-the-Moment
"Birdie, girl, don't josh around foolish
like that ... it sounds insane"
but a statement serving only to
make her rush him, slap the wind out of
his backbone and consequently peal off
an even louder guffaw
sounding perhaps like tweety sobs
if you didn't otherwise know her style—
"well you can blame it on that
eagle dream I had," she might say
"or maybe it was the too-many slugs of
Jack Daniels I took in, so it's really
the booze that's laughing"
but not even a torrential downpour outside
pounding on the windowpanes as if
wild condor wings wanting to get in
could stop her ...
the critical moment is here
she giggles her awkwardest-scurry way over
to the cage, opens it for fingers
to snatch up the finch lashing feathers

to evade her ... with wild fluttering
seems to sense its desperate squawking
may be its last—
her enclosing fist vices onto
the fragile body, a sprung steeltrap ...
her loudest grinning cackle
makes it plain that very soon
still another bird
will have to be replaced ...

Definitions Are Also Wastes

LAURA JOY LUSTIG

perversion
is
people
seeking
wisdom
to
spit
back up
to
UN-
service
areas

Definitions Vary upon Sizes and Substances of Heads

LAURA JOY LUSTIG

balance
is
(to me)
on
off-centered
beams
(wobbly)

Lost enemies

MARK SONNENFELD

Lost. enemies   [to—draw—suit]
zoPt   and oth—
              grrr
      gone

Avantegarde . cup , some nervous , gauze curtain
    'Drip Faucet' It:
and: g minor scale-play the dead flower
[cat shapes] + [Because Listen to repeat]

       the sky every

. Nobody quite understands a — . '
. Literary retooled war path
. Corduroys
. Weakness throws and thought-silly
. Subtitle
. Earphone metallic voice opera and yet
. **' Reading '** it all See windbirds via

      for hours reproach

Sneaking Up on the Enemy

SCOTT GORDON

they plucked their eyes out of their sockets
held them on by the tips of their fingers
and peeked around the corner

"there's the way to do it"
we agreed
each one of us wondering
why we'd never thought of it before

johnson popped his pelvic bone back into place
kerzowski wiped his pecker with some leaves
as the sarge motioned us ahead

i mailed my last postcard home
dropped acid
and prayed for rain

the prehistoric birdthings soared overhead
and the bombs echoed through the streets

the horizon converged into universe and
the universe funneled down into death

bullets know not names

Everyone Has to Have a
Reason to Live in Order to
Live Mine Is the Jungian
1 Where the More Pain
You Endure the More
Pleasure Will Come.
Life Is Pinnacle Pain

she's waiting
to
die
& i can't
blame her.
what else is there
besides
what we've already
seen before/
life
w/ all its UN-necessities
breeding vexing itches
&
vibrating
bone
like matter
in an undisturbed
motion
that has no end

w/ 1 simple trite
anesthetic
where 1 simple
death
can cure all/
or at least
tend
more
possibility

Of Convicts

DAVID "MALACHI" ROBISON

Behind the walls in a prison enclosure
Hidden there from public exposure,
Men endure filth and human brutality
Where nightmares exist in cruel reality.

Treated like animals: cheated and abused,
Their talents and skills are shamefully used,
Where sadistic guards exercise their whims,
Condoned by superiors who encourage them.

Every day of prison in a convict's life
Is made to be one filled with strife,
Wherein he is doomed to forever be
The hapless victim of misery.

There in a world of bitterness and sorrow,
Men live and curse their tomorrow,
Enduring a torment made harder to bear
By the knowledge that society doesn't care.

For they are criminals—it's undeniably true,
But they are also human, too,
And being human they deserve to be
Treated much more humanely.

If I Could Be a Part of Your Body, What Part Would I Want to Be ...

CHRISTOPHER J. KRANZ

I would want to be your hair because ...
I want to rest on your shoulders, and whisper in your ears
I want to touch your soft skin, and see your pretty face
I want to be taken care of—softly, gently
I want to grow strong in your hands
I want to rest above you and protect you
I want to grow with you and do what you do
I want to be a part of you
When you sleep, I can touch your soft, soft lips whenever I desire
I can see all of your sighs, and share all of your feelings
I can be with you forever

Sweet-Talk Days Waned

JIM DEWITT

the morning's final racket of reconstruction
has leaked itself away from
December's streets. ... "when can any
like-laughter sounds replace the jackhammers?"
Frankie sighs aloud to no parrot
or goldfish. ... but caution:
one cannot be certain of horses being spooked
by rattlesnakes, or neighborhood rosegardens
going berserk spilling stalks
across sidewalks. ... beware—
what makes Frankie feel it's now
speed-walking time, away from the blipglitch
of her childbride existence?
but her pullover's been ripped
from her latest smacking session
when unashamedly she'd blurted to God
in a universe-vent—
now the sole sound disappearing
is steel wheels somewhere, screeching away
on steel tracks ... as she stumbles herself
off the lowermost step, sunglasses flying—
rage? no, regret ... or self-blame?
but none give near to satisfactory excuses
through this dark December tunnel
she must try to flash past, while the from-nowhere
thought keeps sticking in her head
"why don't honeysuckle vines try to choke
the streets anymore
under thunderheads moving thither?"
yes, Frankie has to slip out suddenly
to glance at everything, anywhere, except at "him"
in this chill of mid-morning
the sort to make horses' ears perk—
"consarn" comes her mind-alert's burst at realizing
she's left behind the very yak's wool cardigan
needed most, but defies her body
not to return for it. ...

perhaps shivering will tough things out
till some steaming espresso
the Such-and-Such Diner ahead serves up
the surest cure for any cold air's rush—
just then a trash truck with its unique non-quiet
passes, splashing, jarring re-reminder
of those jackhammers as her boots behold
the Michigan Slush Season
surely begun, one further disgust
inserted into her life

You Realize

Former sad delusions stick,
And I am reminded of when my mind was thick
With cobwebs, stagnant and thick like mud,
With unhealthy hormones in my blood,

And each complex can come back to you
In idle times, for they stick like glue,
And perhaps when you are trying to sleep
They rise up and form a turret steep,

But pleasure without pain cannot be,
And from shapelessness does grow symmetry,
And a frog does turn into a handsome prince—
It is just that learning does make you wince.

The evening's levity is no joke,
And you listen as you drink and smoke—
You watch with eyes reflecting fear,
And you realize there is sickness here.

Bowling Alleys Are as True as This

LAURA JOY LUSTIG

nails are
bitten
on.
pink ladies w/
billion dollar
poodle perms
continually
exist
& existence is
often too much
4 s/.
there's a cadillac
in vegas/
pregnancies w/ pigs
happen
in homo sapien uteri
while lover's
gone
awaiting-jury-duty-drills
while
suspended
human officials
impregnate pink pigs.
as we watch 4 mystery
fruit baskets
like no other kind.

Losing Sleep

GIOVANNI MALITO

Couldn't sleep last night. Was out
with the boys. Had a few beers. Shot
the shit. Someone asked—Can you
remember your very best climax? And
I'm still awake, thinking. And I'm
beginning to worry I always will be
because I can't even remember the first one.

His Connection with the Universe

LAURA JOY LUSTIG

like life
cock
too
is
hard

Sunlight

MARK SONNENFELD

SUNLIGHT.")
THEN CAME A DAILY ACTIVITY, BUT IN A
DIFFERENT PLACE PHAEDRA SMOKES
CONTAIN CARBON MONOXIDE
'FRIENDS'
APARTMENTS AND OFFICES, I SNEAK IN
IT'S ABOUT IDEAS, IT. ...
THE INSTRUMENT PLAYED LIKE IT BE
A BAD RUSSIAN IN A ROLLER RINK

———————

THEN   THE LATE SHOW I SLEEP A LOT
                    (BUT) GETTING THE MOVIE
        (IN) camera angle(s)—it is an instrument—
(that runs through the cemetery)
(dawn is the <u>GHOST</u>),
        LOCAL MUSICIANS
IS YR CREATIVE ELOQUENCE
16 INCHES FROM THE CEILING

YOU SURE) YOU DON'T HAVE
BLOND ROOTS, MOST OF THE
BRAIN CELLS HAVE TOPPLED
FROM A FORKLIFT, THE INTERVIEWER

STAYS IN A SAFE little room with a (guard) after

7 o'clock (she's) a real buzz-saw

Remember Me

CHRISTOPHER J. KRANZ

I might be forgotten
Lost in your mind
To remember me will be difficult

When you see me,
See me in the sunlight
Of the end of a good day
In the petals of a rose
In the sounds
Of a love song
In the strokes
Of an artist's brush
For there is where I
Remember you

Days of Hunger '93-'95 (Sung to the Tune of "Me an' My Concrete Feet")

SCOTT GORDON

call me from your better place
wrap my ears in butter
sweet sounds
birds in the background

i'll wish you well and smile
wiping fresh ice
from the window
looking through it—
prism
crystalline promise
once upon a time
perhaps

phone me from your better place
send me some soundbites to treasure
gimme something to chew on—
audio bone bargaining
with the queen of deceit
evil female icon
soul stealer
angel of piss
who's now soaring

giftwrap
a well-rehearsed story
it seems
the least
you could do

feed me the almighty progression
of your vocal cord vibration—
it'll sustain me for months

i'll more than likely tap lightly
on orphaned photo albums—
velcro grip
of the past

still smiling but not really knowing why
shuffling through four or five c.d.'s
etched with your image
bearing your name
conjuring you
in the darkness

Waiting in Hallways While Death Springs in the Right Season: Sithing Morbid as Usual

LAURA JOY LUSTIG

life is hard.
i love things
hard.
because i'm
too soft
& remember everything
& death faces/
empty eyeballs
staring through
harder things
than
life.
life is boring
when yr not living
& most folks
pass on the utilization
of air.
living takes guts
—i've spit up
plenty
& know
what i got.
so
i feel
confident
when striding
& spitting
"go fuck yr'self'z"

to those
in great
need
of good
fuckings

Paraplegic Puppets of the Noodle

LAURA JOY LUSTIG

never be saved.
results are often more troublesome
w/ anus-driving
overachievers
& clever personality
mutators.
be where you know it is.
wherever the is
is
that you love to atomize
because destruction
was assigned gene
in pools of
no-say-splicings
& ordinary suspecting victims.
be where you know/
where cement semen
slide like wet bananas
off forks
of all things sterling.
lick only
what & who you wish to be licking
w/ turbulent tongue
of under-exposed maelstroms.
when all looks like no control
it's b/c we're often w/o/
prospective buyers watch
industrial thighs clench
no matter what the cause.
because cause is
dead
spitting up next 2
swollen returns.
response is

living-sick-futile
questions w/ answers
of "don't know's"
& care less's
of its all powering & pissy
popularity
among curious folks
which killed
more than s/ cats
that search 4
things missing
b/c they know
they cannot be found.
metaphysics keeps them busy
in avoiding substantial evidence
in truth cases
of all kinds.

assuming

(assuming)
a pimple on the nose
    MONIKA
    eyes' by

guilt trips has a 50-50 chance

or more!
fun summer afternoon
Understanding?

(a)
(b)
(c) time goes by—
(d) you're a poor listener so then
       bitch-motives play it mean
       2nd guitar!

My Scars

GIOVANNI MALITO

I have been too much
the romantic, trying
too hard to be gentle,
dressing you slowly
in tender caresses,
coating you with kisses.

It isn't enough—
you want my shirt
and you want it now.
So go ahead and rip it.
Rip it from my back
and leave your scars.

Super-Living in Breathing Skin for Better or Worse

LAURA JOY LUSTIG

i'm super
living.
sunk down
& swallowing things
smooth
w/ mass & me
popping
up
s/x'z hard
but all x'z
biggest
w/ greatest lovers &
uncalculated
anatomical
ledgers.
super living
comes
in
& w/
cozy sweats
& certain
ward-off
permitting moments
of minds
when guards become
confident
& coronary
equipped.
it doesn't happen often
but the
coming

up
is super living
heaven faded
& fucked the
true
lunatic
smiling
buying
nothing
& watching it
be
the better
deal

3 Short Fictions

MARK SONNENFELD

1)
       2 full days plus evenings, though:
       it hurts my teeth
       that song
       to non christmas decembery writing
       it's going to potatoes for dinner equiv.

2)
       THIS IS NOT A STUDIO FOCUSED
       on a direction
       so really word got around
       people
       show me
       how he spilled the bike
       a pen grooves a little harder
       is like the chorus—of mine walking
       down the red house stories
       few people understand
       about self hiding

3)
       delirious
  . . . . fifty folding chairs
a dimitri street basement, adjacent rooms
these are observations.   I am stuck.

Procrastination

J. J. CAMPBELL

i put things off constantly
always saying
i'll do it tomorrow

and when tomorrow passes
there is always
the next day

and it keeps going
on and on

and i realize
that one day
there will be no
next day

for which
i am grateful

that someone else
can put these things off
for me

Lament 36

SCOTT GORDON

never got a postcard
but i never got the blues

too many clovers to press between pages
too many secrets to discover in the dawn
too many truths to seek out
within the invisible bounds of madness

fidget around plasma-like
in the dark womb
called insanity

West Europe

MARK SONNENFELD

supplemental on pamela theme
                    1979
                    (book)
bad on four drawings: outwards
                    to 108 centimeter
this shape a leaf in part
italicized friendliness.
(8's   conceptual   okay   a p2
   —trenchcoat   nightmare dark
a floor polished anna's number in its own special pocket)
a world complexity
a play, be the scarier bedpost raindrops?
ADJ6715 is the license plate.   put the heart
into   it soft shoulder   w/sketch
of power stations synchronized
other places fictionalized a hint of
strangeness?

pls to send
by black ink
a small flat address in belgium
                    (when the 4 means
              of transportation) (the factories on river
           her hair, surroundings)
         (the halfday-off when not caring to shut up
a special dislike
the department of restricted) (is not mine)

The Beauty in the Bull

MICHAEL SEAN CONWAY

torn by the horns
on the last passing,
the Bull regains form,
and charges again.
in the Matador's eyes
you see death approaching
while the cape conceals
the mortally wounded man.

Don't Beat Yourself Up about It

GARRY BANKS

... He's been acting pretty strange these last few days ...

... Rambling on and on about not being able to control his hand ...

—Nyko! Stop pulling my hair out!—

<u>Nyko</u>: No, let me finish. It looks good. It's a new style ...

The Dream and You

LINDSAY WILSON

for Annie Marie

... and there you are
on the edge
of the dream and physical
like lucid curtains
turning
　　　turning like an S
in the bedroom
between red and yellow light
between what I dream
　　　and what you are
the same, but better
because I can touch you

On the Shore of Luck

J. J. CAMPBELL

sitting here wondering
if i were meant to understand
or even be understood by
these people
these masses that surround me
mindless, motionless
lifeless bodies drifting along
these murky waters
hoping to wash up on the shore of luck
and it makes me laugh
because i've spent the greater
part of my life
trying to separate myself
from these masses
yet i know i'm the same
just another
fucking waste of potential
just another taxpayer
going to work and coming home
avoiding the evening news
hoping that somewhere between
the cigarettes and vodka
beethoven and miles davis
i will find that escape
something like a great old movie
only shot with better film.

Lay

GIOVANNI MALITO

I followed her
to the dancefloor
foreplay
      and later
she followed me
home   where
she burned away
under my breath
escaping
      before
she had even
asked my name

I Will Never Die, if You Never Forget

CHRISTOPHER J. KRANZ

The times we spent together
may seem to fade away so quickly

But on gilded wings our hearts
will soar high above

And keep in mind the love
we shared that kept us warm
on nights so cold, heart to heart

Keep this love in your mind
and we will both grow old together

And remember,
I will never die,
if you never forget

Fork in the Road

J. J. CAMPBELL

it's good to see my cat
out in the yard
chasing the mice and birds
pouncing on the leaves
licking her ass clean
she seems so alive at times
but as i look around this house
the empty bottles of whiskey
pages of poetry scattered around
book after book waiting to be sold
for gas money
cigarette money
beer money
i can't help but think back
to some fork in the road
and i can't remember
if it was me
or someone else
but i definitely can say
it was a fool
that told me to go
down this path
this road not chosen by wise men
and i am forever
fucked because of it

The Story of Hamm

MICHAEL SEAN CONWAY

@ first there was
the egg: let's
call it Hamm.

one day, the egg
broke open, and
Hamm Omelette
was born.

Hamm lived
a scrambled life,
often felt like
an old egg salad.

Hamm felt like
he was waiting
on someone
to put him
on a cracker,
and finish
his ass off.

Hamm could taste
the botulism
in his blood.

E7, A7, B7

MARK SONNENFELD

E7, A7, B7

My blues-note is some natural and flat key of Cmi eights—
I go nuts, I attached to simultaneously
        Dreams   on the verge

Ummmm, And I thought . . . Anything,
               I thought of getting
                   A word out
This is going to working—

Much less, It is as simple as that
I thought, And in the world who'd
              Understand?
IN MY PLATFORM UNDERSHIRT
SLATE MY PERSONALITY DISORDER

HELLO?
cemetery arm jacket, muds, the soft snow
visible at what angle a marble-confessor that are built
is to the street

KEEP
to the surface phenomenon on private farm, a car
it is black. Oh come now it is written
on all the aspirin boxes, Dr. symptoms, coffins committed a patch
a porch light is on over a ways, a pitch, a sound,
a frequency everyday bombed.

After Last Call; Or, What I Always Liked about You

LINDSAY WILSON

for Robin

The wildflowers are almost out
under the waxing April moon,

and you said, "We have to amuse these people,"
and came into the Starmart with me

to buy a single pack of condoms.
The woman behind the counter blushes

as she needlessly tells us
to have a good night.

Morning Psalm

MICHAEL SEAN CONWAY

Give me a golden joint to smoke
     in the easy hours of dawn,
before the sleeping world awakes
     and their mad rat race resumes.

Give me a rich cup of coffee,
     and some poems to open my eyes,
to settle into the day
     'fore the mayhem of noise arrives.

Lament 23

SCOTT GORDON

there's no contest
for syphilis.
there's no *Brady Bunch* scene for that.
no halo reward
for the muted parade
of anonymous
infectious
disease.

na-na
na-na,

na-na
na-na,

hey hey hey,

goodbye.

A story began with the idea
MARK SONNENFELD

A story began with the idea.
Very high clouds in step
with crickets, mice, underground vegetables.
It is a quieter living-room couch with
clothes on the hanger

smoking a joint
and staring at our toes in time
to catch the bus.
As it sounds
the dialogue verbs I wrote
don't fool around in the local jewish cemetery
pocketing the here and now necessary
sight of the sodium shaker.

# Jass

GIOVANNI MALITO

Tut tut I say
wag that finger
sway that head
from side to side
not up and down
like the rockers do
because this is jazz
and you know where
it comes from
don't ya?
the word I mean
it comes from Creole
New Orleans
and Algiers cathouses ...
jass is what cats do
when in heat

GARRY BANKS

_____. ... I went crazy and they drug me here ...
... The End ...

_____: Um ... yes ... well, surely you can go into a little more detail, can't you?

_____. —Don't call me Shirley ...

"The Number You Have Dialed ..."

LINDSAY WILSON

You're a voice
not even live—
a pre-recorded message
on an
answering machine
telling me lies
in advance
like: "I'll call you back"
or
"I'm not in right now,"
and I've become
questions,
but your machine
doesn't answer a thing.

New Theme for the Twenty-First

run deep,
run
solo.

The Simple Joys of Insanity

MICHAEL SEAN CONWAY

i look out the window and see ...
there's magic in that.

a Mexican sunrise slowly lifting
its lazy lids over this desert.

after staying up all night long,
smoking buds while sipping down
aqua de piña w/a quart of vodka;
i feel ready for a snooze
@ the dawn of creation.

the roosters are crowing;
passing cars increase.

one more smoke,
and i'm outta here.

I'm (comma)

MARK SONNENFELD

I'm (comma)
look at this picture
now step back on it
it is a nightmare
to assemble
people must tune-in like a junkie
it's got a hypodermic needle
in it
an alzheimer complex
or a lack of dimension
or a lack of blood to the brain
the white clay definitely
has helped
see I was just to a point
where I was about to walk out
the door
there
wrapped around let me show you
life on in a room
(everything here)
of
don't want you to take me in
the wrong thought
in e-minor

Shards of the Past

Doors slammed shut creak silently in the wind
Time's warming breath eases the pain away
and the creatures bury memories deep in the forest
Among the shards of dreams long gone,
a vine grows, reaching up to that empty space—
filling it with new dreams and hopes
The past, now broken, brings blood to the touch;
a painful reminder and lesson of youth
Yet I return to touch the pieces, hoping
that the end was not so near and clear

Aspiration Means Nothing

LAURA JOY LUSTIG

i one day
aspire
a certain
freedom
that ascends
drink
(to suck
strange dick).
i aspire
1 hr.
to not
have to
learn baseball
to become
UN-single
& s/1 else
much like
those
i
snarl
at

Ed electronically

MARK SONNENFELD

Ed electronically

Or documentary

At 0% dB.
Out of the wind, THE
But a list to zero pointing
I do-nothing
I get the picture
I get out of my bag

A standing pattern on a twoway street
Laundry sounds hmm, Well
11:00 a.m.
What I owe.　　　　Others that have no need.
Things my own　　　　　　　　dumb-smart . . .

mathematically-out

basically to lose

engine power

My Life Doesn't Have to
Be like Yours & I'm Not
Sure if That's Good or Bad
but Know That Not Caring
Is Good Not because You
Chance Broken Hearts but
because It's Too Much
Useless Stuffing for the
Turkey on Your Neck

LAURA JOY LUSTIG

life is
s/thing I know
nothing about
& do
very little
of
w/out tremendous
complications
b/c it is
a gentle
UN-thing
meant not for

observing
but gently
paddling thru.
the quiet x's
are the best
x's
—most resembling
longer periods
of space
than
x.
it mimics
unsweetened & precious
herbs
on
impure
1950
t.v.
x.

What We Become

LINDSAY WILSON

... and then one day
you're moving,
sorting through
those boxes
life becomes,
phone numbers
on candy wrappers,
bills paid months ago,
torn newspapers,
insurance ads,
magazines and catalogues,
funeral notices and
wedding invitations,
notes to your lover,
1 Uno card and
a score card
from a game you lost,
receipts
that don't add up
to you.

To Be Sung with a Silly Stammer

MICHAEL SEAN CONWAY

let the world carry on
in its own silly manner,
let the ships strike 'bergs
till we begin the world anew.
let the King and the Queen
fall on their ass and stammer,
cuz they ain't nothing but soft
cake-eating fools.

Toothpaste on Bloody Panties

LAURA JOY LUSTIG

toothpaste
on bloody
panties
becomes
titles
& divorce
or admiration
doctrinals.
differences
are rarely
calculated
in manufacturers
of ends/
becoming signs of
comforting
relationships.
preparation includes
scrubbing
torrid blood-filled
panties
before laundromat folks
get there 1st.
can't take chances.
mustn't live so hard.
busy yr'self
cleaning house
& panties/ practice
perfection in
preparation skill
mastery
4 laundromat
eyes/
spontaneous
landlord visitations/

proper
disallowance
of denuding
truism
& disillusion
of what truly
is
comforting

3 a.m.

hum
buzz
plop
drop
shrill
whistle
kettle
boiled
and
my head
about
ready
to
explode

Bachelor Pad

SCOTT GORDON

... step out onto the balcony.
my invisible donkey platform
has wheeled out more whiskey trauma,
more one-up tequila cockswings,
more intense wiggling
than the lot of the city combined.
fate calls me by name,
i am one with the fabric of the universe
when perched on the precipice
dangling like imminent saliva
from the gargoyle's chin.
(i'm constantly swinging into oblivion
constantly down with desire)
the automobiles whistle and whine below,
crunching bodies with plastic seduction
and bludgeoning the will to transcend
the common & obvious syrup flow.
happenstance junkies flood the sidelines,
yearning for the metaphorical cum-shot,
crooning for extinction
in the bowels of another earthly night.

19) My Letter X

MARK SONNENFELD

a dead body is a dead organism.
a cork bobbed in the water.
         the atomic clock, communist
      haircuts
persons/
the whiskers influence
12:20 (something, as
to cause (blood) to flow)/
looked-up number 22
photog.
metalwork (sometimes fol. by)
the sunlight motionpicture of disease,
the news of departure
to murmur   a picture representing this
      two handles on a cup—
      whose job is it to locate missing persons—
      every year seems another branch is dried up—

Irony of the millennium

PINGUINO

Two paths, and one less traveled by
Which has attracted more attention
Why is it that the tougher road
oft leads to poverty and desperation?
Where is the happiness in suffering?
Is artistic merit worth the daily
pile of flavorless noodle on spork?

What is punk, when you buy the beer
and smokes that own everything
and everyone you yell against?

Reception on life's TV is fuzzy;
the big picture is lost—
Only the work of the individual
is fully understood by that person
A chunk of our life falls out
The guts of civilization gone to shit

Two paths, and one less traveled by
Both owned by the same city
Both controlled and regulated
It's all cross-referenced
with multi-layer dollar signs attached
You, too, will be bought and I
will laugh and throw pennies at you

Martinique

ZOE A. JAIMOT

If you are white
living on this island
is like drifting away
on a happy lilypad painted
by a drunken french impressionist
all about pastel feelings
hiding in the make-believe
easy currents of a blue-green world ...

If you are noir
being on this island
is like learning to speak
la langue française those
extra letters and accents
hang on every word
which kicks and caresses you
strangling tongues with controlled cliché ...

In the Cards

PAT STEELE

We sit cross-legged
on your bed and drink
Richard's Triple Peach from water glasses.
John watches us swallow with disgust,
yet there is something soothing
in the blue room,
the cheap wine and Smetana
coming over the radio.

John leaves and you uncover
the Tarot deck.
You lay out the cards
and apologize for your predictions,
but everything you say rings true.
More than a little drunk,
I light your cigarette
and trace my hazy future
over the cards
in the smoky, cluttered room.

Extinct

MICHAEL KRIESEL

Maybe
we're

the last
ones who

don't drive
convertibles

and eat
cheeseburgers

the last
Neanderthals

who'd rather sit
down on the ground

paint our bodies
with the sun

teach our babies
how to sing

& You Wonder Why

HOWARD P. GUIDRY

... buckwild juveniles/lost with no time to find themselves
can't think on an empty stomach pumpin puffy till
the sun comes pushin
awake still hungry w/no platinum Jesus Peace
just them innercity streets/ghetto stardom dreams
and the T-Lady in between huffin and puffin with 4
mouths to feed.
skipp't elementary
learned @ 13 ah Quarter Cane = $$$
and the only real consequence is the pen where
1 in 3 blk men at anywayz.
anywayz, "Got to be a man," got to grow up fast
when kick't out of shelters for having
too many siblings
& no job, or when you can feel the bones
in yo/baby brotha's ass when you hold him.

makes ah "Grown man" cry
makes ah juvenile find a 4-five on a blind
course to freedom.

& you wonder why. ...

Down on your luck

GIOVANNI MALITO

You sing notes unaligned
and you dance a cliché.
Predatory accidents
are looking for you.
Your machine travels
without any breaks.
It swerves on murderous curves.
The air moves too fast
or too slow for your intake.
Forsaken, you hop
the express tension train.
Your eyelids droop in the drone
and they fall past your nose.
Even in the sunlight
pink translucence is illegible.
It has been several hard days
and long nights of existing.
Your friends have deserted you
having come up on their luck
while you sink down under yours.
But it doesn't really matter
if you just stand on your head
and shake your feet all around.

Pennsylvania War

ASHLEY GATEWOOD

Finding peace with myself,
As the war between us rages on,
Has put a hole in the stockings of this little girl.
Doing it to myself again.
Dwelling not on the finish,
But the end.
It's hard to sleep alone,
Especially when I know you're not.
You've gone to steel country, mining town.
I've got a mind to steal your heart and keep it in coal,
To burn it until the embers have gone out,
And a peace treaty is signed.

Childhood

B. Z. NIDITCH

The white trees
have banished you,
beside ice branches
you are alone
in your backyard
the sky makes you dizzy
yet you want this morning to last
even if the pebbly sun
exposes itself
wanting reconciliation
in the snowy light
and you run against
the east wind
in the fur of winter
nothing will exchange
the knee-deep desertion
of your childhood
nor will you make room
for your shut-eye conscience
of a buried street angel.

Angel Kisses and Bliss

KARL CHAMBERLAIN

Not one to sit sadly
in my cell, I imagine

Joy

fashioned from simple
things: a toothpick

flosser, baby shampoo,
and water. Together

we spin iridescent hues,
spheres of rainbow light.

Shivering with delight, this
dance amuses the angels that

sit on my shoulders, laughing
at a fool who dreams of angel

kisses so light they tickle
my skin and float on the wind

like a child's laughter. These
bubbles pop, but softly, leaving

sudsy echoes of laughter,
joy that can even be felt

from this Death Row cell. Stop
and look again at whatever is

blown in the wind, whatever life
gives you. It is a gift touched

by an angel's lips. Sometimes the
dream passes; sometimes it remains.

But angel kisses and bliss outlast eternity.

Choice Argument

JIM DEWITT

Joye Rhyde's pique
is seen dishing out silence.
Conglomerate of past cephalic angers
piled up. Non-muttered clutter
haunting two otherwise bright lives.
Could it be the consequence
of a once-hot love?
So stand arms akimbo
watch both show puzzlement.
Today's non-collision
with any soft bed has become stark
reminiscent of a Lost Eden.

Pointing Your First Finger at Somebody

JIM DEWITT

like a gun just doesn't terrify
anymore. Though t'was of yore
such gesture combined victory with smirk.
But now what's in
is slashing fingernails across
your jugular for dire effect.
Uglier at expressing mojo than Nietzsche
would have been, when you wish to go for
blacker butchery.
S & M dismalitude was never
more vogue. To showing off
crime de la crime nightghoulishly to
every degenerate technitron
who's into bodybag chic.

Shareworthy Subjects to Germinate

JIM DEWITT

poetastry morning breaks out as a half-
rooftop cassette of cloudlessness
facing at that baker's dozen of banyan
trees obscenely spreading gams and
crotches across mudflats dinless with
tidepull not even one day in advance
to be appalled at by the lying legends
of local charlatan "writers" so thus
back-of-my-mind inspired I polish a
few new-wrought tales appropriately
loaded with Petered Panns & Meddling
Mummies & Fantasy-Figured "Ladies"
all to be vociferously related flambé
at the verynext coffeehouse soirée ...

Watching Nicely Nudity

JIM DEWITT

Blatant body parts
plainly inhaling/exhaling
the real-you-before-the-fall ...
revealed not because
clandestine curiosity must check up
on "natural cycles"
oh no ...
it's (personally) my love of
observing True Life fluctuate
predictably around
physical nature's parallel lines.

cloud girl

KEVIN M. HIBSHMAN

reclining horizontal.
won't you shapeshift
behind a puff of wind?
grazing the blue emptiness,
drift above me.
i salute you in passing.
the silent dignity of formlessness,
i marvel.

cloud girl,
now darkness pregnant in the storm
of your belly bursts forth
as a million tears weep and
the flowers drink from your
bittersweet giving.
fearsome cloud girl,
mythical is your mystery.

heaven's hip barmaid

KEVIN M. HIBSHMAN

sister,
for a season
we hung.
crazy girl,
haunted by her own
fierce intellect.
a huge hunger
words cannot express.
we were only trying
to outrun the end.
still, i see you.
blue hair.
black dress.
a walking bruise
to remind them.

i could die here
in a haze of menthol.
your spirit near.
we all die waiting.
heaven's hip barmaid,
please save my place.
if you end up there.
if i end up there.

nostalgia

KEVIN M. HIBSHMAN

seething prettily in shredded black.
decades have rolled over me.
i am a lady of style.
i collapse like a cardboard box
to the consuming beat of a song
no one can remember.
i glitter here in the corner,
tiny vestibule of your mind.
despite the hollow times,
i shine.
spit is the sheen.
i gleam in my dream of refined decadence.

can you read the signposts?
i am not vanished nor will i.
i delight, sealed off in museum light.
i abide by my own code of wasted elegance.
i thrive.

My Son

SHELLEY KRANZ

for Chris, 1980-1997

You came to me
during a time in my life
when despair was all I had

From that moment on
my life became *real* and *full*
I finally had a
reason to live

I gave you life
by bringing you into this world
but you, too, gave me life,
a reason to live, to prosper
to feel whole

You, my son
are why I am here

You, my son
are why I am today

You, my son
allowed me to gain self-confidence
and to better understand the world

You, my son
gave me hope, encouragement,
trust and inspiration

I loved you then
I loved you throughout your life
I love you now and forever

Lightning Blues

CATFISH MCDARIS

While sitting in
my shrink's
parking lot

I watched a magnificent
lightning storm and
swirling gray monsters
in the sky

In the distance
was a freeway
They have always
been an ominous
phobia for me

Taking pills does
no damned good
I still can't drive
upon them

I guess I'm just
one fucked-up
individual

Walking around on
a planet of war
death hate love
alligators punks
bikers dogs shitting
in yards rapists
child molesters
cops with handcuffs
eating chocolate
doughnuts

And here I am
crazy as a
motherfucker
waiting for pills

There is no cure
for what I have

Not now not ever

Do I give a damn

Fuck no.

Suicide Blues

CATFISH MCDARIS

When I was in the
Milwaukee County
Mental Ward for
my attempted suicide

On my 50th birthday
on July 29th, 2003,
I met a young pretty
woman who was 23 years old

She was extremely
agitated and had
death in her eyes

She could not sit
in one place for
over one minute

She said she had 9 children,
4 at one time

This seemed impossible
and was most likely
a drug- or alcohol-
induced lie

She told me she
had given away 8
of her children
and stabbed the
eyes out of her
3-year-old son

I didn't believe her
but there were lots
of things that have
no explanation

She got me in
trouble by
smoking my pipe

All the tobacco
smokers were led
out to a small
caged patio

On the patio
was a post
with an electric box

You pushed a button
on the box somewhat
like a lighter in a car

A coil would grow
red hot enough to
light a cigarette

Since I was the only
one who smoked a
pipe, I required
matches

The guard would stand
there while I lit my
pipe and take
the matches from me

Like I was
a pyromaniac
or arsonist
I could tell
he feared me

The young woman with
the tale of the maiming
of her child wanted
someone to screw her

I think a guard
or doctor obliged
her

After the guard saw
me let the woman
smoke my pipe
through the
observation
window, I was
informed that
my smoking
privileges
would be
taken away

So I stashed
tobacco and
matches in my
sock and made
a pipe from a
soda can, I
smoked in my
room and thought
fuck the guard

I watched the
patients smoking
like caged animals

Sometimes it was
pouring rain

They all smiled
thinking I was
suffering without
tobacco

All I can say
is the nuthouse
is a bitch

Only jail is worse.

A One-Legged Ass-Kicking Contest

CATFISH MCDARIS

I drove near the school
to pick up my daughter
and her friends.

This man about my size
was throwing chunks
of ice at children.

I yelled at him to stop,
he shot me the finger
and nailed a kid in the head.

I got out of the car
and said, "Hey, that's
enough." He ignored me.

I took off my size 14 steel-toed Wellington,
he cocked his head sideways
like a dog that hears a canine whistle
beyond the range of human hearing.

He grinned a step-onto-
my-web-said-the-spider-
to-the-fly evil grin.

The boot I held jumped behind his ear,
I punted his nuts about 50 yards' worth,
he sounded like a rat meeting
and eaten by a pit bull.

"Why didn't your old man
just punch him out?"
"He doesn't believe in violence,"
my daughter explained and snickered.

Round 8 (in an electronic information age, Greek tragedies come in all forms)

ZOE A. JAIMOT

I pick up the ringing telephone
and it's instant madness.
Who's that! Who's that! he yells.
Infuriating to think who would call me
as his footwork moves him closer to listen.
Rage pounds behind his eyes blinding him
in possessiveness choking off
any meaningful communication.
He regards me as an ornament
of conquest to do with as he pleases.
I try and dismiss this round of threats
with a practiced turn of my back.
Hoping to ignore the impending drama.
The way boulders in middle of rushing streams
succumb to the water's constant slap.
Merely enduring immutable nature.
But then again natural aggression
is seemingly a sparring game.
Get off the phone! He spits through
a mouth tightly drawn like a boxer
waiting to finish with a brutal flurry.
Thumbs tighten over knuckles white
in fisted manic rage. My body
still bearing fresh marks.
Bruised and beaten oozing pinkness
in spots like the color
of a cat that alternately licks
and then bites until it is frantically raw.
I squat in the darkened corner holding
onto the phone as if it were a lifeline
of polite conversation and escape.

Hoping he will never check my computer email.
His eyes dog me like a thief.
The scent of oppression and terror
always in my nostrils.
He stands there like a conqueror
waiting for me to stroke his body
and then bend my being to its hardness.
How many times has he jerked some dress—
over my head leaving me without face.
A perverted pleasure of hateful excavation.
I can taste my fearful breath
and it sickens me like sour milk.
And in that instant, I can see
a mare lying in the snow.
Strangled by its own umbilicus
which is still attached to the foal
while life bleeds away
into coldness as stark and real
as wiping my own blood
from the porcelain bathroom tile.
Wrong number, I say, rising and walking
cautiously past him as if at the end
of another round when pugilists halt
their feral beatings by agreement.
Always wary and on guard as I
calmly replace the receiver
waiting for the next combat to commence.
And he believes he has won again.
Never really seeing my eyes
or the slight smile of resolve
like an empowered Clytemnestra waiting
to slash out of that shadowed space.

Le Sel Noir—the black salt

ZOE A. JAIMOT

Venus and Serena Williams win the
French Grand Slam Doubles Championship
at Roland Garros Stadium, Paris, June 6, 1999

Two sleek Black bodies dominate this center court.
Barriers, even gentle mesh tennis nets, that divide sides

are never benevolent. Chip and charge. Volley and serve. Back and forth
these dark women, beads jangling from long rows of flying hair—

which look like amulets: small bones, shiny precious stones,
charms woven in braids to protect both from evil. These women

streak across an artificial surface as if their body muscles
flowed and contracted like free-flowing African rivers.

Two proud young women, taking life by the throat with the aid
of tremendous serves and syncopated movements as coolly choreographed

as any by Bojangles Robinson—these women who would have been
just trophies for Ebo warriors in another continent of time,

worth many heads of cattle, chickens, arable fields not like
in this civil society where both will never have to worry

just where their next pair of sneakers or the next new Mercedes
is coming from. While TV commentators lob praises like warmup hits

between teens who battle for unbeatable forehands from polycarbon
racquets as youth passes when minutes tick by in matches measured

by shouts of "Fault," "Doublefault," then "Out" echoing from judges.
Murmurs passing through the crowd about unforced errors and sins

of the fathers visited on daughters as passionless officials wearing
designer sunglasses sit high in chairs judging what was up until now,

a game dominated by ponytailed opponents with perfect tans.
White girls outfitted in sweatbands, color coordinated with pastel

towels as they blot perspiration from soft skin while their youth passes. Minutes ticking away in matches measured by blurring overhands.

All these women to keep loose before a return swaying and then bounce away from riots transferred from rap CDs on drug-infested streets as if

bigotry could be eliminated through sweaty effort. Undoing our geometry of sameness in this unforgiving dance of adolescents playing the match.

Listening to these two Black women occasionally shriek and wail bringing back shouts from a different era of mothers crying for babies ripped from

protective bodies when slavery and subjugation was an accepted game. These two Black women staking out their claim to not mere equality.

Delivering meaner strokes slashing inside lines which cut as sure as hateful words. The N-word and worse, which are said under breaths

flicking net tape to drop forlornly as hope from lives of these girls trapped in adults' ego to win endorsement dollars and top-seeded rankings.

But two Black women, defy our bias, knocking back what appear to be sure winners with crushing ground strokes that do more to improve

perception than all the trash-talking of activists espousing political agendas to please followers who measure life's achievement in court control.

Two young Black women, like all the rest of this legion of tennis girls, systematically leap on left legs to wallop crushing serves as severe and

deadly as any act from a female Medici. Committing acts of service and conquest to please family, friends, and countless fans. Winning matches

but only accomplishing momentary draws against prejudice. For to some, their very presence here rubs and stings the wound of racism raw.

The Big Boy

I see him out there alone in the parking lot
grinning through hazy July afternoons and
snowy January nights. He's the Big Boy,
the statue holding up a giant cheeseburger
in front of the chain restaurant that bears his name.
In my dream, I unbuckle his red and white overalls,
and we become lovers. His lips are warm and sweet
as cherry pie fresh from the oven, his embrace vital
as morning's first cup of black coffee. I wake up
naked, my mouth tasting of chocolate milkshake,
feeling so good I don't even mind the ketchup
stains all over my favorite sheets.

The Veil from Her Face

DAVID J. THOMPSON

Years ago now, in the high mountain valley
where they sent me to teach, the townspeople agreed
the village prostitute had a daughter,
though no one claimed to have ever seen her
without the veil she always wore. Half believed
she was an angel, sent as a sign of God's mercy;
the other half argued she was a monkey, the devil's own child.

One late autumn Sunday morning, I packed
some treats and went to find her for myself
in the hills where they said her goats were pastured.
Vaya! she yelled as she saw me approaching and threw
a rock that whizzed by my face. Tranquilo, I said,
soy amigo, as I continued slowly toward her,
showing the almonds and chocolate I had brought.
She crouched, but didn't move, snatched the food
from my hands as I knelt before her.

When she finished eating, she caressed my hand,
let me slowly pull the veil from her face.
Her eyes were dark diamonds, her hair blazing black,
gorgeous beyond words, a young Ava Gardner.
Below that, though, she had the nightmare fleshy nose,
coarse lips, and toothy grin of a chimpanzee. I pressed
her hard against my chest and ran my fingers
through her hair, felt her begin to unbuckle my pants.
When the church bells sounded in the distance,
I told myself to keep my eyes closed and remember
to bring plenty of bananas in the weeks to come.

A Give and a Take

ANDY URBATS

unwanted,
and intentional:
there are ways
to be alone.

like digging into the ground
searching for time murdered,
and slowly letting the grass
die.

like vacuuming a floor
deep in old smoke and piss,
and opening a window,
letting it all drip out like waterfall
for only a few seconds.

like letting a cigarette burn
ashes and punched out
upon sitting glass on the table,
and taking that one final drag,
coughing it out
and
smiling.

like the last drink
lucky and later
puked out.

like the smile from a lonely and old woman
greeting you at the 24-hour supermarket
handing you this week's specials
at 3 in the morning.

a rabbit letting you feed it.
a cat slowly crossing the road
without cars
either way.

a man at the register
spotting you the 15 cents
for the cigarettes in order
to make
the change even.

a give,
and a take

and no more
than the other.

Frognosis

CAT CALDWELL

They were terrible to animals.
On the Texas ranch, after a good rain,
the frogs would come out.
They'd shoot the frogs with BB guns,
or stuff them full of firecrackers
and throw them up in the air.[1]
Ker-pow!

Gandhi said,
You can tell a lot about a culture by the way they treat animals.
St. Francis said that, too.
It's been said that boys who torture animals
are more likely to grow up to be serial killers.
Or American Presidents.

Someone once asked me: How could the German people have let
the Holocaust happen? I would never have been complicit in the
torture and murder of so many people.

And I think of the man in Abu-Ghraib
with electrodes attached to his crotch.
And the one who was beaten until he passed out,
was revived by an army doctor so he could be beaten again,
revived, beaten, passed out
revived, beaten, passed out
until he died,
a phony death certificate all that was left.

A third of my paycheck goes to the United States government.
I have supported the oil cartel with every penny I have spent on gas.
We are those German Citizens of the 1930s.

---

[1] *Kristof, Nicholas D. "A Philosophy with Roots in Conservative Texas Soil." New York Times. May 21, 2000.*

I remember hearing that if you put a frog in a pot of boiling water,
he'll jump right out, but if you put him in nice lukewarm water
and heat it up slowly,
he'll stay in until his skin falls right off.
Aside from trying to figure out why
anyone would want to boil a frog to death,
this is nature showing how
a situation can become lethal
and we won't even realize it
so long as it's just a little bit worse
every day.

Acceptable nukes?
Acceptable levels of arsenic in the drinking water?
Acceptance of secret trials, or holding a person indefinitely
without charging him with a crime?
Acceptance of the torture of prisoners of war?

I have a friend whose father used to beat him every day.
His father went to prison when my friend was 13,
and he'll be in for another 20 years.
Fuck him, my friend had said, I hope he dies in there.
My friend was in the marines until he got kicked out.
I'd have gone to Iraq, he said, I just wanted to kill people.
What he really meant was: I'll never be a victim again.

In this country
we live in anguish, anger, and fear.
For good reasons.
Like 10,000 handgun deaths per year.
Like 10,000 nuclear warheads.
Like how almost everyone I know had a shitty childhood,
and almost every woman I know has been raped.
Like a frog in a pot of boiling water
Like a frog in a pot of boiling water
Like a frog in a pot of boiling water

You can tell a lot
about a culture
by the way they treat
the animals.
Gandhi said that.

But Gandhi also said this:
When some British official asked him,
Little man, do you think we are just going to give you India?
Gandhi said, Yes!
And that is exactly what they did.

I know a small girl who believes she will change the world.
And she will.
Her dad, my friend, said,
All I wanted was to kill people,
until I opened my eyes to the fact that
there is no hope but that which we make;
I made peace with myself and with my father;
I could never kill anyone, now.

They were terrible to animals.
But we don't have to continue
to let them be terrible
to humans.

motion

CHRISTOPHER WISE

I need to take something apart.
Let it be complicated and messy.
I want to see piles of screws and gears and circuits
laying across my floor.
I want the scratches and scrapes on my hands from digging
prying and ripping out the pieces from a machine.
I want to use the wrong size screwdriver on the right size nail.
I want to trace the line on a circuit board like I'm looking at a map
to somewhere I haven't been before.
I want to yell and curse the one piece that's stopping me from
getting at the motor at the heart of the machine.
I want blood flowing from under my fingernails from where
little bits of solder have tried to fight back or find a new home.
I want to hear the sound of plastic cracking under
the duress of my wrench that has become a hammer.
I want to feel vertebrae like pop of metal being wrenched
from its secure hold.
I want to see my fingerprints made in the grease from the gears
that would be lined up by size and rank along the wall
waiting for something, if anything.
I want to run electricity the wrong way through what's left
to see if it sparks or smokes.
I want it not to fold and give up its secrets willingly.
I want to be surprised by the blood from the cut I didn't notice.

The Roses

ANDY URBATS

Oh great heaving lighting sky
downward
upon me,
take glance and be what judgment ultimate.
when it is hot
and yet I meant to cool
let the tree fingers wave their cool hands to me
and let me wave back
as my hair will surely soothe its agitation softly.
when ill-minded heads find my shoulders comfort
let the ever-greatness lift them
and drop them under the hard-paced walks,
every day frenzied tap(crush)ing asphalt—
hot stinking betrayal to good will
and spiritual progress,
let the ashes raise steam spirals
all
around
the sins
of the sinners.

Oh great infallible question
educate my answers
so i may ask more and again
with blind frequency
and a love for back pages.
may unacceptable behavior,
and people and situations,
may they accept what they are not
and move as I have for you
of you
to you
due
to
you.
let them know love as longing
for as i have loved.

Oh fixer of broken remedy
take this recipe and add you something something.
take this body
and form the vase around it
case it
and stick your fertile hand
to guide the roses.

straddling the boney death

PATRICK McKINNON

my boss at the restaurant
gave me the old pep talk
again this morning
another one starring hard work
as manna in the desert of poverty
onto which he was born
sed he always wanted a new car
& now he's got two always wanted
his own house so now
he has a house a cabin & a condo
on the gulf coast sed he wanted a boat
& now he's secretary of the yacht club
told me i got what it takes
to manage this place
maybe even buy it someday
if i keep my nose to the stone

& i said i know what you mean marv
i was born in ethiopia
& didn't eat my first meal till i was ten
thot i'd be straddling the boney death of africa
for the rest of my pathetic life
but one day i happened upon this ad
scratched into the bark of a withered tree
WANTED: YOUNG GIRLS TO SUCK SAILORS' COCKS
& EAT THE RAW SEWAGE DRIPPING DOWN
FROM THE LUXURY CABINS OF A LARGE CRUISE SHIP
BOUND FOR NEW YORK CITY

i knew it was my only chance so i did it
slept in a small box w/spiders & rats
caught v.d. & gangrene & rickets
but made it to america & got a job
as doormat for an elegant hotel
scraped together enuf money for a sex change
& a skin transplant & finally
once i was good & white & hung behind
a fat-headed penis i came in here marv
& bullshitted you into giving me this job

poem for my neighbor who lives in the building across the lawn

PATRICK MCKINNON

what is she reading my young neighbor
out in the lawn chair wide white hat
tipped low over princess makeup so i
cannot see her eyes as they follow words
in a brain synaptic fusion
between the author & her
& shes somewhere far away
from the twenty yards between us
the trees & bushes conceal my window like some iron gate
birds fly thru dawdling w/branches
fluffing wings & body feathers my neighbor
turns page after page but her face continues
holding the same flat motionless expression
either this book is an empty concrete wall or
my neighbor is a statue whose mind is disconnected
from her facial muscles then suddenly i notice the spine
of the book its writing from the pop singer jewel & it
whips me back to last night when i
lenny bruced a mondo urban street fair
an audience two solid blocks of hats & heads
by reading graphic poems about the awesome joy of cunnilingus
& the crowd was myriad vocal explosions
a raging mouth roaring grand approval gross disapproval & the
cops shut me down wouldnt allow me back on stage
were gonna arrest me & my poems for disorderly conduct
until i told them it wasnt conduct it was art
so theyd have to arrest me for disorderly art
& that would become a scandal i wonder if my neighbor
in chartreuse & pink bikini vogue blank lips & cheeks & jaw
absorbing the hackery of the highest paid poet in american history
was in the audience last night w/her boyfriend or

her girlfriend i wonder if we had any fusion
of the pictures in my pen becoming the
pictures in her head & if she was there
if this did happen did her face respond
w/some kind of movement did she smile
did she sigh did she frown did she shout
i want to go out to the grass & ask her but
its minnesota rain begins & my neighbor
retreats into her building as
many birds take shelter outside my window &
the lawn is an unbroken vivid august carpet once again

love poem at the end of the world

PATRICK MCKINNON

i want to unzip yr jeans
slip yr panty elastic aside
& feverishly lick yr labia

now

i know the world is ending all around us
like some people even have
a specific date in mind
& bombs are being televised again
falling as usual fracturing communities
so exactly similar to ours but

i want to gently peel you open &
linger my tongue along
trembling tender inner thighs before plunging
into the rubbery pink of yr clit i

realize the air is choking on chemicals while
garbage & petrol & fertilizer are
clotting the water & enuf of us
are jacked on caffeine & emotionally in need
of something on sale that the
industrial commercial carnival continues
gulping the soil upon which video children
will never play but i

want to nibble that rosy button
high heat between velvet skin make it
wetter than its ever been feel you shiver &
twitch in the first throes of coming then hold you
there & hold you there & hold you there i
want to be slurping
yr vagina slick hearing yr moaning
yr gasp yr sighs when

nuclear light ignites the sky
or a stray comet
strikes mayhem from outer space
or suddenly food disappears
in some worldwide laboratory-induced drought
or bugs overrun mankind
in surreal multiplying militarizing moments
or whatever grim catastrophe
awaits this shadowy pustule
orbiting a fever sore
in the disease-ridden mouth called universe i

just want to be tongue on crotch
lip to lip slathering w/nectar
suspended from my eyelash tips sweet darling
ride these taste buds forget the maniacs
even on franklin avenue right outside this window yes
sirens at night w/my head piked back in yr naked lap
are dream angels octaves above us
enviously decrying our indulgence in this ecstasy
i want to lick yr labia love im
gonna suck you silly

His Eye Is on the Pyramid

NEAL WILGUS

I
G.W.
Bush —
Not need
explain you.
I'm Qommander.
See, I like kick
ass just for hell.
Butt we're all on it
together, you know —
peace is our confession.
But the bottom of our line
is class war welfare — buck
the rich, fuck the poor, screw
the rabbits, let's invade a bunch
of places so we can keep a taxonomy
jolting. It's the stupid scheme they
tell me — but down deeper, it ain't no
warming globalism, ain't no faiths basis:
It's oil, oil, oil, oil, oil, oil, oil, oil, oil,
It's an oil, oil, oil, oil, oil, oil, oil, oil, world !!!

The Master Always Answered the Question

HARLAND RISTAU

the troubled novice,
Where would you go if you
were not certain where to go?
Lin Yu,
Some place else.

Stanislaus Is a Cauliflower

JIM DEWITT

Stanislaus catches the tail of her eye. Pellegra quickly becomes a suctioning butterfly, draining him thoroughly dry. Spent, he is not immediately sorry nor does this even surprise her. The words "bungling mistake" do not flash anywhere even for a fraction of a second.

Without slobbering off so much as a drop, Pellegra routinely sweeps her sado-equipment into an oversized carryall that he stares at but is unable to move toward.

And she waits ... patiently for Stanislaus to at least fumble for some syllables of emotion, just anything gutfelt ... even if growled coweringly ... be they stock-cliché phrases from the anti-rush currents of his mind. But when hearing none come, Pellegra edges gently through him into the thick wool of her own object-oriented feelings.

All bedroom walls seem to be saying "no regeneration right away, so time to go" while a remnant of their latest familiarity hangs from the foyer ceiling. It suddenly suggests to her the open door to evening, while back across the carpeting detects a slight grin of chagrin from Stanislaus.

Now outside, the bright summer night lines the streets for Pellegra, beckoning, would be tolerable if ... when just then a passing red sportscar honks fortuitously in her direction, pulls alongside for her swinging into the hard palm of a bucket seat unaided. Instantly the chest belt clutches her with its life-threatening leatherness. She becomes a frivolous young girlie giggling in a playground swing as a callused hand massages acceleratingly into the split of her femininity. Reflex raises Pellegra's knees as if pleadingly. Quick positioning and strong shoves seem very aware of her cryingmost need. But being careful not to crinkle her face-obscuring skirt. It had apparently learned its lesson on a prior night such as this, long before she had first felt helplessly the primal rise and fall sounds so hard on the ungiving ground.

Then the city sees again the red sportscar clipping along at ninety-some per, proof this night has not been wasted. But meanwhile, what of Stanislaus back there in the bedroom? Still mesmerized? The very thought-occurring of it launches Pellegra up over the car door's glass panel. She feels an undulating speed for several seconds before it happens ... one of those rare moments when her mind totally focuses her body, enabling her to bounce back into the very waiting bedroom she had quit.

Voila, their words rejoin. It is the trigger for Stanislaus. His smooth hands-of-doing begin more craftily, at last comprehending true de-sire. And Pellegra has anticipated and is responding. ... All of their encumbering abstractions have evaporated.

He sees her suddenly-knowing smile reveal how she is playing "the taker." And as if for videotaping their enacted scenes of joy+pain are festooning furiously. ... Nothing can stop this lecherous bed-dance. ... Hear the cheers. ... They've scored!

Ode to the Seeker

GIOVANNI MALITO

for Albert Einstein

Sailing in a ship without prow,
without preset course or defined direction
but for the hazy aim of a oneness with the sea,
the seeker grasps for everything
at once, a nothingness
for it is the same, absurd desire.

No knowledge can ever be complete
and the seeker does know this,
but he would perish if not for his struggle
and his planting of hope
in the fallow fields during a famine.

Someday he may be forced to succumb
as countless others have before him
to a windfall bliss, ignorance in the end,
but it will be a violent submission
for even as no seeker ever finds all,
all seekers must refuse not to find
for all learning is life-yearning.

quoting silence

where there are humans
you'll find flies,
and buddhas
—Kobayashi Issa

i was fresh from the street
i met a buddhist poet
i wrote with many words
he wrote with few
i said many things
i said nothing
he said very little
he said all
i said
"words are the poet's
tool"
he said
"words are the enemy
of the poet"
lao said
"true words are not
beautiful. beautiful
words are not true"
we stared at each
other in noisy calm
chiang shih-ch'uan said
"a reflection
appears on the water
then is gone"
many flies
many buddhas
nothing
all

why buddhists don't kill bugs

NORMAL

don't kill him!
the fly it wrings its hands,
its feet
—Kobayashi Issa

i am dedicated to all insects
that call my name
that keep me awake
crawl on my face
stick their feet in my stew

they have not forgotten me
never
never in my life
certainly not in death

unlike perfect bliss
they will remain

they will be here
to serve
to praise
to take my shit
to eat my shit

to let me know
in no uncertain terms

i shall never be alone.

the riot

on the street that day
three of us were beaten rotten

one woman was raped beneath
a pile of overturned garbage cans

a child was hit by a motorcycle
that jumped the curb

an old junky from detroit named pete
had his eye scooped out with
a linoleum knife

somehow i managed to escape
unharmed

was it fate?
was it the star of david around my neck?

what it was not
was survival of the fittest

for that was the weakest day of my life.

fighting for love in the afternoon

the wife grew bored
the hubby was uninspired by golf
they both grew tired
too lazy to cook or do dishes
breakfast was skipped, lunch & dinner called out
talk fizzled to brief comments about commercials
she did phone gossip
he did internet porn when she was out of the house
he cultivated a slow-rising beer belly
she grew hemorrhoids like mushrooms in the dark
the sunrise chilled
the sunset dappled
the peach tree in the yard blossomed
the fuel of summer ran out
outside their shaded window
the mailman left his letters
the children came & went
pine fragrance crawled over the rooftop
inside, the fog enchanted
the lotus fought for survival in the mud.

Colophon

The edition you are holding is the First Print Edition of this complete anthology publication. It comprises several previous journal issues and anthologies, published as individual chapbooks and photocopied books without ISBNs, spanning from 1997 to 2007, with single straggler pieces from various projects spanning from 1993 to 2013. The included publications, now in paperback for the first time, are: *Crackrock #1* (November 1997), *Crackrock #2* (August 1998), *Real-Life Poet* (January 1999), *The Literature Collection* (July 1999), *Punctuation* (2002), *Broken Livers & Broken Lives* (1996–2006), *Avenues & Parking Lots* (2006), and the Myspace online netzine *Medusa* (2006–2007).

The cover and title page fonts are set in UglyQua and Old Newspaper Types, both created by Manfred Klein; 4990810, created by Phillip Cavette; and Avenir Book, created by Adrian Frutiger. The interior titles are set in Chase the Sun, created by Stasia at Call Me Stasya, with the author names in Alpaca 54, created by Andrew Hart at Sick Capital, both used under a full commercial license. The back cover Alternating Current Press logo font is set in Portmanteau, created by JLH Fonts. All other fonts are set in Athelas, created by Veronika Burian and José Scaglione. All fonts are used with permission; all rights reserved.

Cover jacket artwork created by Leah Angstman. The historical curtain graphics are in the public domain. Back cover spotlight image by Angelie Mejia. The Alternating Current lightbulb logo was created by Leah Angstman, ©2013, 2020 Alternating Current. The Violet Ray logo was created by Leah Angstman, ©2020 Alternating Current. All artwork is used with permission; all rights reserved.

The editors wish to thank the font and graphic creators for allowing legal use of their work.

OTHER WORKS FROM
Alternating Current Press

All of these books (and more) are available at
Alternating Current's website: press.alternatingcurrentarts.com.

alternatingcurrentarts.com